The Butterfly House

"A wonderful poet maps her life – and its imminent end – with candour and love in one of the most astonishing feats of poetry you might ever read. This is a collection written at the furthest edge of the world, reminding us what it means to be alive – sunlight and the Atlantic, of course, and also misogyny, and grief, and snails. Throughout it all, Kathryn Bevis is luminously present, inhabiting characters and scenarios so various and unflinching that when she tells you "I want to be here", you feel how deeply and fully she means it. Let the gate of your heart swing wide open. Read this book." – *Clare Shaw*

"*The Butterfly House* is an explosion of a book, crammed with bright imagery, experimental form and surreal backflips. Tiny clockwork hearts rub against parties at the end of the world. Bevis takes her place as one of the most interesting and vibrant poets of her generation. Superb." – *Joelle Taylor*

"Kathryn Bevis is a great love poet, and I don't use that word lightly. Her greatness is both in her vision and in her gorgeous poetic abilities. I prefer her poem 'Love' to George Herbert's of the same name, to which it's a worthy successor. Bevis's imagination places cancer in nature and makes it sexy, thrumming with beauty and part of a a wondrous, wild evocation of life. A stunning collection." – *Gwyneth Lewis*

"*The Butterfly House* is a collection of poems which is without precedent. It's one thing to say that poems are brave or beautiful or full of love, but to read this collection is to learn anew what those words mean. Kathryn Bevis is a poet who can do anything, now inhabiting the voices of superheroes, teddy bears, rivers, now drawing sustained metaphor from the natural world in a way that allows us to feel our connectedness to flamingos, penguins, whales, now swaying us through a line's gorgeous music, now opening to the vistas of beautiful long poems. And the thing is that all of this technical mastery is serving the highest purpose – the poem's emotional impact, and a world-view that is suffused and glowing with love. As the poet writes, 'every poem I write these days becomes/a love poem,' and rarely can poems have flung their arms so fully around the world, or shown us the world in a way that makes us want to do exactly the same. The result is a collection like none I've read: these are poems for everyone and for all time, which hold out their hands to everyone who needs them, which are answers to the questions we didn't know how to ask." – *Jonathan Edwards*

The Butterfly House

Kathryn Bevis

SEREN

Seren is the book imprint of
Poetry Wales Press Ltd.
Suite 6, 4 Derwen Road, Bridgend,
Wales, CF31 1LH

www.serenbooks.com
Follow us on social media @SerenBooks

ISBN: 978-1-78172-755-3
ebook: 978-1-78172-761-4

A CIP record for this title is available from the British Library.

The publisher acknowledges the financial assistance of the Books Council of Wales.

Cover painting: 'Heartfelt Thoughts' by Catrin Welz-Stein.

Printed in Bembo by 4Edge Limited, Essex.

We are all one question and the best answer seems to be love
— a connection between things.

MARY RUEFLE, *Madness, Rack and Honey*

Contents

After

Before

My body tells me that she's filing for divorce

She's taken a good, hard look at the state
of our relationship. She knows it's not
for her. The worst thing is, she doesn't tell
me this straight up or even to my face. No.
She books us appointments with specialists
in strip-lit rooms. They peer at us over paper
masks with eyes whose kindness I can't bear.

They speak of our marriage in images:
a pint of milk that's on the turn, an egg
whose yolk is punctured, leaking through
the rest, a tree whose one, rotten root
is poisoning the leaves. I try to understand
how much of us is sick. I want to know
what they can do to put us right. She,

whose soft shape I have lain with every night,
who's roamed with me in rooky woods, round
rocky heads. She, who's witnessed the rain
pattering on the reedbed, the cut-glass chitter
of long-tailed tits, the woodpecker rehearsing
her single, high syllable. How have we become
this bitter pill whose name I can't pronounce?

Soon, she'll sleep in a bed that isn't mine.
That's why, these nights, we perform our trial
separations. She, buried in blankets, eyelids
flickering fast. Me, up there on, no — wait —
through the ceiling, attic, roof. I'm flying, crying,
looking down. *Too soon*, I whisper to her warm
and sleeping form. *Not yet. Too soon. Too soon.*

After

Everyone will be there

in their tea frocks, their slim fitting
suits, their lumberjack shirts, their sequinned
skirts. They'll arrive in their dozens by wagon,
on horseback, in cars and on unicycles, shod
in their heels and brogues, their spats

and chunky trainers. Amy will have manicured
nails. Dillon's buzz-cut will flatter their face
more than they know. Everyone will come
as themselves. Noah will untie bright balloons
from backs of pews and we'll watch them rise

to bob on the vaulted ceiling. Rosa will trapeze
from arch to pillar, from gargoyle to crest
to scoop them up in shining armfuls.
And there'll be cake, more cake
than you've ever seen: custard slices,

black forest gateaux, a Victoria sponge
with cream, raspberries and mint,
a lemon drizzle drenched
in elderflower syrup, French macarons
in fancy flavours — rose and pistachio,

lavender and orange, almond and fig.
Everyone will get to eat their favourite
cake. It's going to be delicious.
Lucy will invent outdoor games and Matt
will win them all, though there'll be trophies

and medals for everyone. Then we'll play
with a huge parachute and there will be no
winners, just a silken circle held
in all our hands, on whose whirling centre
we'll bless the babies, bouncing them in turn.

I'll be there, wearing a wicker dress.
Friends and relatives will braid in my bodice
a meadow, bright-tipped with the names
of their love: angelica, bluebell, cotton grass,
dog rose, eyebright, forget-me-nots

(of course), foxgloves and — hell,
why not? — a huddle of real foxes.
There'll be goat's rue but no goats
on this occasion. There'll be heather
gathered from the easy body

of the moor. Purple irises will stick out
their yellow tongues. Jupiter's beard
and Jupiter himself will RSVP.
There'll be sea kale and lady's bedstraw,
meadowsweet heady from summer's lanes.

There'll be nettle. Margie will plant
on my yoke the oak she grew from an acorn.
Jon will strew pear blossom, queen's crown,
ragged robin; Vicky will wreathe silverweed
cinquefoil blown backwards until it gleams.

In pride of place, Ollie will thread my skirts
with the thrift that clings to rocks
at the Brough of Gurness, stitch in
hedge parsley's umbels, Mum will sew
a pink fringe of velvet grasses

to my hem, stud woodruff at my cuffs.
And because no common name
for a native plant begins with an x,
everyone will kiss and blow kisses
instead. There will be yarrow. The smallest

of us all, James, will drop the last
flower, a zigzag clover.
I will blaze with love's colours
on this, my parting party from this world.
I want it to brim with rapture

for everything my tongue will not,
by then, be able to christen:
cockle locket; hagstone; the slight
plosive sound my love makes as he falls
asleep beside me; the shock

of sunlight through a window like yolk
on a willow-patterned plate; the way
every poem I write these days becomes
a love poem; the way I've written 'love'
six times in this one and won't stop;

the way the name of each person
I love is part of a map that traces
the contours of my belonging,
each name the answer to a question
I didn't know how to ask.

My Cancer as a Ring-Tailed Lemur

We both know one day she'll eat me.
But, for now, we dance: a little game
of catch me if you can. Tracking her
is difficult. But specialists are interested
and, bit by bit, they creep inside my body's

forest, stalk her with their fancy cameras,
take images, write reports. On ultrasound,
she's punk-rock stripes of white and black.
On mammograms, she sunbathes, downy
as a dandelion gone to seed.

The child I am divines the time by blowing.
Five years, ten years, twenty, more. That's
when they spy her, up in the canopy,
her tail Rapunzel's plait looped
round a single sentinel node. Now, on MRI,

they spot her kindly spaniel's face
crammed into the lettuce of my breast.
At last, on PET-CT, they catch her
on the move. She's up and off alright: a lope,
a leap. She careens through my branches,

omnivorous for bone and liver, brain.
Because her nature is to double herself
again, again, she and her sisters huddle, tails
conjoined, tiny arms about each other's necks.
The child I am learns to prophesy afresh,

blows one year, two years, four years, five.
Friends say *this is war* and I'm a *warrior,*
a tower of strength. But the lemur and I
get on okay. I figure she has a right to be here.
She is, in some important sense, endangered too.

I draw the line at poisoning but let
the hunters starve her, most days. She looks
at me with orange eyes of ire as we witness our
habitat's destruction. My new need for naps,
my breathlessness – for both of us a forest fire.

The Butterfly House

i.m. Ray Holloway

Yours is the only death I've ever known.
We sat with you for hours and stroked your hands.
And though it was January — the pond
a frozen oval — though each blade of grass
had etched itself against the ground and each
frail thing had hidden from the stalking frost,
a butterfly flew to your window, sudden
and strange, with wings that throbbed like a heart.
The day we buried you, we saw another: crimson
sails unfurled, its body putting out to sea.

Today's a pilgrimage. I rest in mist and heat.
Red lacewings gather their silk skirts as I trace
a swallowtail's trembling pulse. Together,
apart, together: a pair of blue morphos shiver
like black-fringed scraps of sky. Clear as leaded panes,
glasswings feast on nectar. They close themselves
like hands that meet in prayer, then open up
to cup the tropic air. Since my diagnosis,
I see them every time I close my eyes.
Their flaming wings. Their too short lives.

Anniversary

Today, I will burn up the old year, scatter
her ashes to the wind: the thickened ridge
of flesh she placed in my left breast, the tiny
indentation — a dimple, really, so nearly
not there — so nearly not there, the lump

the GP couldn't find. I will set a match
to sleepless nights, to mammograms
and MRIs, will walk on the glowing embers
of reports, results, the dialect of tumour,
mass, invasive ductal carcinoma. I will

cremate the failed canulations, my hand
slapped to raise a vein, the iodine that spilled
a Rorschach blot into healthy tissue
it had no place to be, the biopsies,
the bruising, waiting rooms, the waiting

itself, the day the surgeon looked at me
and told the truth, her tired eyes, the quiet
room they took us to, its sofa sagging,
the nurse that softly came and went, the Kleenex
on the table, how we knew and didn't

know, how we knew and didn't know.
I will take a torch to the pills, fatigue,
infections, late-night trips to A&E.
Even still, with our heads together
on the pillow, now, the way we hold

each other and gaze, hold and gaze, drink
in each breath the other takes, the cat's tail inked
on the blanket beside us — a question mark,
a metaphor — you're on my list, too. The joy
of being here. The joy of being here with you.

Drug Rehab vs. Palliative Chemo: A Service User's Comparative Analysis

At the chemo suite, there's no creeping
inside your skin. No itching for a fix.
No need to check both ways before
you walk inside the building they've

at last consented to treat you in,
though you've begged them to help
for almost a decade. The years have not
revolved about you — suns around

the Milky Way — as you sit, using,
in your rented room, trying and failing
and trying again, as advised, to *sweat
it out* yourself. You don't need to hide

the signs from those who know you,
those who sense a story here but not
the what or how or why. There are no
compulsory groups, no having to share,

no-one asking you to relive the trauma
that ignited your appetite, the nonstop
friendly fire of your craving for a substance
that sets your life alight.

Here in the chemo suite, everything is calm
and kind. Pain is measured. It is inevitable
and not your fault. Here, you have *courage,
strength;* you wear no shame. No shame.

Imagine that. Of course, there are days
when an ache will spiral from your spine until
you cannot stand or sit. Days you'll crawl.
Of course, sores will blot inside your mouth

and, yes, your hair will fall. Even
your eyelashes will be lost. Now imagine
the cards, the letters that land softly on your mat,
each one opening its paper throat to sing:

I see you; the crystals and worry dolls
that arrive; the silk nightdress that reminds you
you are a woman, still. Imagine your whole
house filled with the scent of roses, aglow

with pink peonies, all of which are at
their most heady, most blowsy and beautiful
when they open themselves up, as one
by one, so tenderly, their petals drop.

How Animals Grieve

We Google it. Laid on our backs in bed
together, cursed by our tired, three-pound brains,
we search our phones' blue light for wisdom, become
voyeurs of YouTube clips on other creatures' pain.

For seventeen days, a mourning orca
attends her daughter's corpse. She sinks
and hauls the weight of her as if to fetch
the breath back, have her suckle once again.

A chimp will carry her lifeless son for months.
She lets the troop draw close to hold her, hear her
screech. They watch her comb the straw from listless
fur and floss with grass between his teeth.

Elephants know to sniff beloved bones.
They seek to raise the fallen, rock their own
bulk back and forth. Each one waits its turn
to stroke and roll the skull, slow blow

through its trunk, take time to bury its dead.
Like us, giraffes and housecats, dingoes, horses,
dogs forget to forage, forgo sex and sleep. Like us,
at burial mounds, they pace and yowl and keen.

So why should it surprise us, Ollie, — us
who matter most to one another, us whose marriage
is as deep as marrow — why is this loss
unthinkable: me without you, you without me?

This

A fire has been lit in new leaves,
will grow to a green world
in the dark wood. Small whites
rise in drifts to the swish of our boots.
Nothing is worth more than this day.

A pair of grey wagtails fly low,
gold-bellied, over the rushing river.
Their bodies translate water
to sunlight, sunlight to water.
Nothing is worth more than this day.

Here, the wind toys with leaves like loose
change in the pockets of the sky.
High above, a wood pigeon calls to us,
wild and true, *Who are you, who who?*
Nothing is worth more than this day.

Love

will not sit still, be good, make no noise.
She shapeshifts from a bare tree to a wolf moon
to a mansion. In her courtyard we rest, eat oranges

and persimmons from one another's bowls,
breathe honeysuckle's sweetness as it rises,
ripens, circles the iron pergola. Sometimes

love is a great hall where we stand and stare up
at her hammerbeam roof of green oak,
her upper windows unshuttered, where light

surges into the dark's depth. Or love in a tower
leaning out to let down her hair. Or stretching
like a cat, mid meal, making room for more.

Love has her appetites, her poverties. She
is a watch winding down. But love, too, is where
tide and time have carved runes on the rocky shore.

She is a stingray, stealing the show with her high
voltage, leaping free above the bubbles that scud
on the surfaces of seas. Love turns her back

from the ocean, towards the silence of the moors,
she pricks her ears to the stonechats' call,
that flinty *chink*. Love with her arms empty.

Love with her arms full. Her footlights, her scenes.
She will not be accounted for, will not be held
responsible. Love the mischief, the wilful. She finds

us, presses a track to our door, sets up home
in us. Even when the shelves are built and ready,
she will not allow herself to be arranged,

alphabetised. She will not be tidied into the drawers
under the bed. Love revels in her own exquisite
ordinariness. This soup pot. This loaf of bread.

Egg

We watch a wildlife documentary,
learn how emperor penguins take their time
to perform the tender rituals of come
and go. In autumn, he marches for miles:
all rocking waddle, all bib and tucker,
almost too fat for his feet, his belly
full of krill and squid. And when his claws
grow tired, he tumbles, sledges, slides:
a tiny figure in the whole vast tribe
who trudge through icy wastelands.

Who knows how he finds his way to her
or who performs the choosing? The camera
captures his certain strut towards the orange
blush of sunrise on her cheeks, the stripe
of dawn along her beak. Eventually,
the couple press their chests together
— an opal glow — stand still, stand very still,
their necks bent in snowy folds, their heads
bowed and swinging. Only then must they wait

in freezing wind while famished winter
feasts on them, wait for the egg to be formed
— their alchemy of albumen
and keratin. Then they'll take their time
to rehearse the pass from her to him.
They'll have one chance: a single, frozen
moment. Finally, they risk it all.
The egg must not touch the ice or be lost
to cold, absorbed by boundless white.
Like them, we took our time learning

how to love. Now, as we stand with our backs
to the storm, waiting for the light to fade,
we must keep to the faith in what we've made:
a frail cradle, this miracle
of our life together. Soon, I must walk
on my own in the dark. Know that I want
to be here. When I'm gone and the shell
of our marriage cracks, believe that what
we held between us all this time will break
out live and singing.

Barn Owl Exhibit

Oxford Natural History Museum

Who brought you down, Icarus,
your lace petticoats flapping, useless? How
were you weak enough for the taxidermist to expose
your tiny bones, that precious, hollow echo
of yourself within yourself?

Once you were bark, water, mottled,
touched with gold, your wings a whole river
of plumes, the curvature of your beak
a perfect repeat of your talons. Let me
bring you back to life, Ancient, lover

of the edgelands: daybreak, sundown,
riverbank, roadside. Even your face's heart
is compassed by stiff little feathers. Again,
you'll haunt the blue dusk that hangs
heavy in the wood. Bare of leaves,

the songs of trees will give themselves
to you. And when my spell breaks, tell me:
will you still dream of the sudden swoop,
the softest gathering of down against down,
your own sharp questions scritching the sky?

The Witch in a Bottle at the Pitt Rivers Museum Finally Escapes

Centuries have passed since her flight was stoppered
in this bottle's tight fist. It's bright as a bubble,
a Christmas bauble, shaped like the woman trapped

inside. Until the day of my visit: a school group's ruckus,
a shattering, a scattering of silvered glass,
and out she flaps, dark *flittermouse*, up for a peck

o' trouble. Together, we leap and ride through next-door's
drawers, stroke their small blessings: amulets
in the shape of Hands of Fatima, dried sea horses,

charms to ward off the Evil Eye. She wants. She
has appetites. She must see and smell and touch
it all. Taking me by the hand, she gifts me a bead

with a face, crowns me with a gold torc, shows me
shrunken heads in a glass case labelled
with copperplate. But she wants more, much more,

pulls on my sleeve to *gaa oot.* She wants us to gather
bachelors' buttons off the peatlands in late spring,
acorns at *akering time.* She wants to glide out

of here, take to the air, us two, on a *goatsucker's back,*
wants to drink it all in, *swizzle 'til we're fair*
vuddled wi' it. She is teaching me to want until I ache

to comb out her hair, to traipse together invisible,
indivisible in the holloways, to fly on a jay's blue-
barred feather beside my sorceress, my fire, my bride.

Playing Tigers

It's morning. We paint on our big cat faces:
a ground of white with blackened lines, touched
by the orange of Savannah dust. In this mood,
chubby cub, you want to ride on my back,
off, scent-marking our territory: the beige
wall-to-wall carpet, the Laura Ashley three-
piece suite. You grab at my clothes, my hair,

my cheeks. By lunchtime, your sulk is all sun:
an inferno from a cloudless sky. We slink
quietly through the grass of afternoon,
play pat-a-cake with soft paws. I read to you
on the sofa from *The House at Pooh Corner*.
You're dopey now, strokable, wrapping
your body's striped rug around my lap. Fast

forward thirty-odd years: you're nursing
on an oncology unit and I'm here, straight
to stage four. What we both know about
survival is hard won. *Be a tiger ...* you used
to say, then pause. Sis, I remember
your tiny finger held high, mid-air, to ward
off the unthinkable, ... *but not a real one.*

Night-Time at the Aquarium

and the keepers gone to their beds.
The tanks hum. I sleep on a glass
bridge. Sharks cruise beneath me
in a single, sinuous loop.
As they waltz, their gills grin, crescent
moons in the fluid dark. Tonight,

it's the fire cardinals that drift
across my dream's page, fins soft
as poppy petals, mouths kissing
the water, eager for shrimp.
Inside, bubbles rise in reverse
to the motes of dust that fell

in a shaft of sunlight that day
we first touched — lips, fingers,
skin — in the attic's hush. Up here,
I hover and watch their bodies
blush as ours did. They are candles
lit from within. Swirling

their silk ballgowns,
they queue decorously
to watch me back. Their flanks
are fluted glass. Jewel anemones
pulse the spun sugar
of themselves, endlessly.

The Wheel

It begins like this: in January a single stitch
slips from your needles. By Candlemas,
your paintings, shelves of knick-knacks start
to stray along the walls. Tongues wag
at primary school gates. At Harestock Garage,
the cashier muddles up his change.

By the time Beltane arrives, your socks
unpair, your books unalphabetize.
A crowd throngs in your garden,
waits. We stand from Lent 'til Summer Solstice,
watch your bookcases flatpack, your china
thrushes, wrens, flamingos ascend in a great

gust. Aghast, we see the cat cascading
from your lap. By Lammastide, your whole life's
harvest starts to slide. We hold a single
breath between us as we see you reaching
for your man. An ecstasy goes up as he skids
skywards between your arms with the leap

of an electric eel, a bar of soap shot
through sopping hands. By Autumn Equinox,
your house unmoors and sails down Taplings Road.
At the glass, you transmogrify before our eyes
— a white-pyjamaed speck. November 1st.
All Saints Day's here at last.

Our solid ground's unsolid now, our road
a riverbed. Palmists, vicars, wise ones
prophesy by Yule your body will up-anchor,
your breasts untether, right then left.
They say your spine will wander, your brain
uproots at last. They say a slithering

liver will finish off the task. Who
can tell what's next for those of us still left?
Come New Year's Eve, we'll clasp
our children close, raise a glass to old
acquaintance gone, test our lives
with spirit levels.

What the Dead Do

We sit in plush waiting rooms with our own baristas
and soda fountains, lounge in over-stuffed chairs, flick through the pages
of your lives: you building a fire with winter-chapped hands,
roasting a chicken sprinkled with paprika as the fennel braises,

you walking in Crab Wood to touch the old beech tree, you
with the cat stretched on your lap in front of the box. Remember
what I said in those final months, *It's not what you do
but who you do it with?* If I could choose to do one

last thing with you, it would be to walk from Deerness
to Marwick Head again, right at the edge of the earth
where it meets the Atlantic. We'd hear the sea roiling, its nearness,
watch the spray gush from the geo's rocky chasm, back and forth,

as though from a whale's blowhole. Do you remember this:
the scent of seaweed and peat? How I kissed the salt from your lips?

TRANSLATIONS OF GRIEF

Denial

We meet each week. I tell her who I am
today: how, in disbelief, I am a nursery
of sardines. *Go on*, she says, and I speak
of our flicking, cross-hatched skins, our silver,
shoaling bodies, the swallowtail of our fins.
I explain our obedience to the pull
of colder currents, how we dine on blooms
of plankton, how oblivious we are as dolphins
wait to herd us toward a surface snatch,
as gannets mass to fire themselves — gold-
hooded — a thousand arrows to the sea.

Anger

Next time, I'm fury sitting there. Zipped
in a zebra suit, my nostrils flare. One word
from her and my body is a bucking bronco
that never wants to stop. I'm fabulous,
of course — a fashion model with a perfect
arse — dressed to kill in symmetrically
shredded tights. I launch the designer handbag
of myself, thrash my tail and mane, hoof
the box of tissues, boot old Freud and Jung
and Kübler-Ross onto the floor. My kick
has force enough to break a crocodile's jaw.

Bargaining

Friday, midday again, and I'm here
on the dot as a lyrebird on her chair.
I trill. She nods in time to the rhythm
of my tiny, clockwork heart. I'm haggling
today with chirrups, whistles: *What if?*
If only… Why? Rehearsed on the forest's
velvet-curtained stage, I negotiate with all
I've got these days: the song of car alarms,
the tune of chainsaws felling trees.
A beatbox artist on the wing, I scratch
and tap and pop my habitat's demise.

Depression

At last, one day, I come as myself.
The quiet holds us both. I try
to tell about the blue whale I'm trapped
inside. There's so much we don't yet know
about blue whales: how many they are,
where they go to breed. But she knows
as well as me that a blue whale's heart
is the size of a Ford Fiesta: each chamber wide
enough for a drowning woman to pummel
herself against, each beat a deep-sea
detonation, a boom against her bones.

Acceptance

The months strobe by. I shapeshift again,
again, begin to believe in the transubstantiation
of the flesh. Aquatic now, I am a jellyfish
pulsing disco lights of green and yellow,
red. I am a bluntnose shark cruising silently
across the ocean's bed. As my fins grow in,
their flags unwind, I am a cuckoo wrasse
with atlases of blue mapped on my sides.
Finally, off shores of East Atlantic rock,
I know I have arrived. Down here, inside
this mirror world, I am alive. I am alive.

Before

You will survive

like Gloria Gaynor, spot-lit and sequinned
on the dancefloor, singing it for all she's worth
because, as you once said, *she really means it,*
or like Houdini locked in stocks
by his ankles, dangling from a crane.

You will survive like small boys pulled,
thank god, from a flooded cave by Navy Seals,
like Wonder Woman, loosing her ties only
a beat before being splashed across the tracks,
or like an orca, beached and calling to its pod
from the rocky shore, returned at last to water.

You will survive like trilobites, scampering
unperturbed throughout the Paleozoic era
or, if you prefer, you will survive as the peony
trembles on its red stem against the storm, as moss
climbs its way up each bright whip of birch,
as the last bell clings to a foxglove's leaning spire.

You will survive as the gull flies high,
then higher over the hospital, its pale body
guiding the way to Oncology. You will survive
the burn and jangle of your nerves, the spasms
in your throat, the PICC line to your heart,
your hair in clumps upon the pillow.

You will survive the long nights where you wake
and cannot sleep again for pain. Mum, look
at everything that you've survived so far. Feel
how surely the world holds you now, how near.
You will survive. And when you do, I'll be here.

In this poem, your routine bloods have come back normal

You aren't anaemic, you're not referred for any further tests.
Here, there's no colonoscopy, no Midazolam administered
for your discomfort and distress. The radiographer finds
nothing to concern her: no masses, polyps, bleeding. Here,
your biopsy results are benign. Here, you are not cut.

In this poem, there's no need for us to learn how
tumours are graded and staged post-operatively,
or to study your body's geometry of area and volume,
its algebra of variables and unknowns. We don't
have to understand that T describes how far your tumour
has grown, or that N denotes how far the cancer's spread
to your lymph nodes, or that M characterizes how far
it's spread to other parts of your body. In this poem, God

is providential, not just in the general but also in the special
sense, intervening in your life specifically, so there's no
need to talk about what any of this might mean
for your prognosis in terms of the percentage of other
patients at your age and stage who survive five years beyond
their treatment. Oxaliplatin and Capecitabine are still
alien words. In this poem, you are not burned, not made
weak or sick. You don't shake. This poem is a world where
it's always Friday and we take the kids to South Stoke park,
take turns to spin them on the roundabout, run them off
with that chase game they're too old for and still love. In this
poem, you're whole. We're not waiting for what's next.

A Wedding

That day, the thrushes finally fledged.
For weeks, I'd heard his whistled songs to her at dawn:

now-now, now-now, did-he-do-it, did-he-do-it,
then watched her plunge into the hedge, bearing

grass, roots and moss to purl with a busy beak. She stamped
the floor with tiny feet, fed the cup with mud and spit,

pressed her speckled belly to the curve
until it grew the contours of a bird.

As we sent out invitations to the feast,
she laid a clutch of brilliant turquoise eggs.

Day after day, she sat and hatched her bulge-eyed brood.
It was a wide-beaked time. It wore her sad and thin.

I'd see them both, smashing snails against an anvil,
fetching wet meat to their young. Then June came.

As I stepped into my dress, mother fastened
silk-covered buttons with her crochet hook

and the last chick tottered at the nest's lip. I held
my breath. It fluttered, stretched, and flew.

I brought the lice-infested nest indoors to find
a tangle of your hair strung gold against the brown.

We have it still: her parting gift. It stinks — of food,
of flesh. This living mess. This coracle of scraps.

Honeymooners' Ghazal

You teach me the name of each bird, my love,
and I test on my tongue every word, my love.

A redshank now boomerangs in towards shore,
where her water-flute cry can be heard, my love.

At Mull Head's rocky ledge, dark cormorants stand
and survey the white spume churned to curd, my love.

A gannet's beak pierces the linen of mist,
pulling fast an invisible cord, my love.

When a sea-fret blows in from the coast then exhales,
once again you're beside me, unblurred, my love.

A crow in a hood flaps its course into squall
round the cliffs of Deerness, undeterred, my love.

These kittiwakes glide — they trace rings with their wings
and your voice is the air that they've stirred, my love.

Anagrams of Happiness

a gram of &s, after Terrance Hayes

It's in the damp whorl of biscuit-scented hair on the nape
of a newborn or in the mint of Sunday new potatoes which shine
under their lick of butter. It's watching for the phases
of the moon, the intentional way it swells and arcs, shrinks and spins;
it is your breath's humidity in this bed of ours, a solid ship
that rocks us in the dark, or in the steam that rises from the compost heap
on winter evenings. It's in the winking silk of a spider's web against the
        misted pane
or in coffee, sweetened with its glob of honey, drunk outdoors in
        smoking sips
from the Thermos lid. It's in our sense that, whatever happens
now is who we might become, this walk together in the woods, these
        plump shapes
of dripping malachite moss, that fiddlehead of the fern's curled spine.

Song o' the River Itchen

My body knows the way
      to where I'm gwin, has always know'd.
     I knows fen and flooded meadow,
       kings and riots, wet woodland,
         Saxons, swamp.
       At Alresford, I quills up,
      gammocky, hoops doun
    through Cheriton, bears a west
 by way of Lovington, Ovington, Avington.
I knows what 'tis to hold
    chock and otter,
       pipe stem, doll's head, watercress.
          At night, my veins run drunken with the moon.
        I knows the damselfly's ticklun skitter,
      the kingfisher's shot-blue flash
    agin' my banks, the jack-hern's
    spellbound stance.
And I knows what 'tis to be held.
    By Winchester,
    I be but channelled,
    a moated, tamed
    so I roars up
    a froth that tumbles,
    clockun,
    gloxun,
    bluff
    through City Mill.
      Summer evenuns,
        I drifts me easy
          through The Weirs,
        blink bright with gold
          past sun-warmed bricks
        o' disused wharves,
      the flint rubble core o' Roman city walls.
   After a while, I crosses the edgeland
     moors at Winnall.
      Wintertimes, I sees
      the brickle-limbed ghostés
       o' cow parsley, pretty nigh froze

in the act o’ reachun.
At St Catherine’s Hill, I be but smolt glass,
fleet, still. By Shawford,
Twyford, I be a speckle-back,
writhun, brindled,
fit to burst my skin.
Bubbles skate my surface
at Bittern: swimmy,
glimmerun. At last, I be drank
in a wink by Solent seas: quaffed
as quick as empires be.
Tell it out.
Time builds hisen borders
around everythun that lives.
Know what ’tis to be held
by what you hold,
what ’tis to be held
by what holds you.

Hampshire Words and Phrases

quill-up, to rise as water does in a spring
gammocky, wild, full of tricks
chock, chalk
jack hern, a heron
clockun, the sound of falling water
gloxun, the music of gurgling water
bluff, lusty, like a farmer
smolt, polished, shining
fleet, a sheet of water
speckle-back, a snake
brindled, severe, fierce
swimmy, giddy in the head

The title of this poem is "What's the Title of this Poem?"

And the first line explores that question. In fact, the whole
first stanza sets it up, economically placing the reader
in time and space, *Late evening in November's suburbs,*
a light rain, and introducing the poem's triggering subject,
an urban fox, *scratting for scraps in the bin-bag black.*

Next, a stanza of rich description, all *glittering tarmac*
and *streetlamps haloing the night.* The fox's coat is pictured
as *the hot-chilli pelt of three-day-old kebab, the bloom of rust*
on iron railings. Smell is often under-rated, so, *He is the musk*
that marks alleyways behind the houses' dreaming backs.

Now, something needs to happen (and a little soundplay
wouldn't go amiss here, a tinkle on the piano keys),
His brush-tailed cry slashes a trail through star-hushed skies. Then
it's all action, action, action: *Nothing slinks like him, nothing*
bites and slices, nothing ruts and gnaws and stinks like him.

There's enough figuration so that we know it's a poem
we're reading and not some other kind of text, not
a takeaway menu, say, or a knock-knock joke. About
two-thirds of the way in, there's an epiphany, *No-one*
sees as he sees. His flaming eyes sear the dark, and the poem

swivels away from a wry and slightly weary exploration
of its own mechanics into something more unconscious,
more emotionally charged. A fear of — yet desire for —
the wild, the unknowable, is never stated but it's everywhere
from this point on, *There is no-one so alone, alive, awake, alight.*

Then a final image, a piece of metaphorical surprise,
concrete yet suggestive. Clunky exposition at this stage
would entirely derail the thing. As the poem dies, we're left
only with the noiseless, savage page, *No one rips flesh*
from the silence as he can — yes — even to its clean, white bone.

Miss means both *Mother* and *No-one*

The trainee teacher is crying in the loo. This time, for both intensity and duration, she has achieved *Outstanding*. And it's not Jed Simmonds or bottom-set Year Nine on Fridays, period five. It's not the safeguarding training or differentiation six ways for every class. She isn't crying for the Year Ten girls whose names she struggles to remember, so well have they hidden themselves behind long hair, immaculate behaviour, and precisely average grades. The trainee teacher is crying in the loo, her heart a strip-lit cubicle whose bulb is on the blink. And it's not her failure to meet sub-point 4d of the Teachers' Standards that's set her off on this occasion, nor is it the School Uniform Policy or the two-hundred-and-twenty-three books she has to mark each fortnight with rainbow highlighters, colour-coded for feedback, action, and response. The trainee teacher is crying in the loo, her heart a plug of chewing gum sticking to her ribs. She's not crying about the spreadsheets in which she must evidence two sub-levels of expected progress for each pupil, regardless of the child. She's not crying for the boy who mimicked fingering her when her back was to the class, nor for the Head who doesn't know her name. The trainee teacher is crying in the loo, her heart wrung and stinking as the mouldy mophead there's no budget to replace. She cries for let's-call-him Jaydon, Ahmed, Tom, held in isolation for a week because he threw a chair when his dad's parole date was postponed, cries for let's-call-her Aisha, Kayla, Kim, who cuts and cuts and shows her all the wounds, cries for the shrug of the Designated Safeguarding Lead (who's heard far worse than this today), for the twelve-year-olds who can't yet read, for the school-to-prison pipeline, for let's-call-him Connor, Kristos, Mo, slumped forever on the tutting chair outside the Head of Year.

Delinquent

Patrick McCaffery: sly-eyed, greasy-quiffed,
hands sticky blue with the BICs he liked to pull apart
in class, his mouth gobby with the spit he let drop
from the science block balcony on our sandwiches at break.

One assembly, his mam was there as guest. She sat
on a too-small plastic chair at the front, twisting
a tissue in her hands as she told us about the charity
she'd started in her dead daughter's name — a last wish

foundation for kids who didn't have long to live
(so they'd get to tick off one thing on their list). Patrick only
kept his face turned toward the floor, perfectly still,
silent as he'd never been, feeling our eyes aimed

into a sniper's red dot at the base of his neck. His mouth
sealed up for the rest of that day as if with Copydex,
shoulders slumped under his standard-issue, bottle-green
blazer like collapsed scoops of lukewarm, canteen mash.

He's long gone now. Overdosed at twenty six. I sometimes
think of him arriving home that day, how he must have run
upstairs, flung himself onto his bed, how he'd worn on his face
the popped bubble-gum balloon of all our fucking pity.

The Smuggler

She knew she'd need to start off small so took the spoons.
What a boon! Easing silver necks from their rosy, velvet
trays into her tinkling sleeves. He only picked at his
guitar with filthy nails, inhaled another toke of weed.

Next, she snuck out lamps and lampshades, ceiling roses,
bulbs. She stashed them quietly in her boot. What a hoot!
He simply frowned, put on his head torch, watched
five episodes of Top Gear, sucked a six-pack down.

Last week, she slipped the curtains from their poles —
how droll! — then slid the windows from their sockets, bubble-
wrapped the glass and hid their views inside her pockets.
He shrugged, pulled on a jumper, filled his bong with grass.

Today's his birthday and she's carried off the roof,
the rafters, chimney pot. So what? This time, he's shouting
at the wind, fists raised to the stars. It's nothing new, this —
the fists, the shouting, the shouting, fists. She's taken it for years.

Tonight, she's packed up firelight, shadows, warmth and headed
south. Of all the things she ever took, it was her ma's
advice that got her out. She'll reach home soon. Oh, him? Look.
He's still there, crouched on all fours, howling at the moon.

Teddy

Delia suspected that her teddy bear was gaslighting her
but found it hard to pin down when he had begun. Was it
when he said her new hat looked *like an animal crawled*

onto your head and died there? Or when he made her say
'hot water bottle' over and over, calling her accent *adorable*?
How the other toys at the tea party laughed!

Teddy said none of the other bears was good enough
for Delia, not the *best version* of her, the version only he
could help her work towards. Paddington liked a spliff,

Pooh was pretentious, Rupert was holding her back
and Little Ted made her laugh too much and *act like
a crazy person*. Order was important to Teddy.

When he woke her at 1.00 a.m., growling for picnic food
right there, right then, Delia thought that something
was maybe not okay. He made a list of silly words

that she used — 'serviette' and 'settee,' 'toilet' and 'cheers.'
When she began to avoid bedtimes, got puffy drinking
late into the night, Teddy said *there's more of you to love*.

He didn't do snuggles any more. One time, he rocked up
on her girls' night out with the ragdolls, saying her lateness
home showed *you don't respect the value of other people's time*.

It wasn't all bad. Teddy taught her the difference between
less and fewer, its and it's, no and yes. He was good at rules
and there was much that Delia still needed to learn.

How to Choose a Boy

Choose him because he drives a black
Austin Princess with a nest of tiny spiders
hatching in the footwell and leaves
them be. Choose him because he plays
'Shiny Happy People' on his ghetto-blaster,
because he wears patchouli in place
of deodorant. Choose him because
you're sixteen and ready, because
he's small and blonde and beautiful,
because he teaches you to build
a fire, roll a joint, to juggle three
oranges, because he knows the Bible
of your body, its *Song of Songs*, its Psalms
and Revelations, because he knows
how to make you shake. Choose this boy
because when you spin together
on Sheet Common, heads tilted back,
arms straining, and the equal
and opposite forces of your gravity fail —
as they must — you will stagger like drunks,
fall together, tangled. Choose him because
the world will have slipped on its axis, for a while.

The Darkening

It started with glow worms and phosphorescent fish,
their lights blown out like candles on a cake. At matinees,
footlights swallowed themselves entire so we only guessed
poor Gloucester's eyes were gouged and heard Lear shake

his fists against the storm. Momentum took. Bulbs began
to organise, to unionise, downed tools across the globe.
Lighthouse beams refused to stroke the sea to sleep.
Whole tower blocks played dead, their pupils blown.

By teatime, even the blood-lit freckles of TV standby LEDs
had mutinied. Dentists' lamps sat down, sat in, called sick.
We blamed the manufacturers. We blamed the government.
Streetlamps picketed the roads on which they lived.

We knew we were screwed when matches joined the strike,
flints declined to spark, magnifying glasses wouldn't catch.
Oil lamps, tapers, flambeaux took up arms.
Conspiracy theorists had their day at last.

Ghosted by our darkened screens tonight, we are
undone. We pray for dawn's red eye to open, watch
as stars put out their fires one by one by one.

The Clearing

At the heart of every tale there is a wood, and in
the darkness of that wood there prowls a wolf,
and in the belly of that wolf there dwells a man,
and in that man there stalks a hunter and his
growling, wretched hunger, and within that
hunter's hunger thumps a heart to pump his
blood, and in the bloodlust of his heart there
throbs a bonfire of his rage, and in the embers of
his rage there burns a fear of little girls and of
the woman in each one and how she grows
despite his fear, despite the blazing of his rage,
how she swells against the lust within the blood
inside his heart, how she climbs within the
cavern of that hunter's desperate hunger, how
she soars to slay the man inside the wolf within
the darkness of that wood, how she grows, this
little girl, into the heart of every tale.

Wonder Woman Questions her Status as a '70s Symbol of Female Empowerment

All my villains like to tie me up. They lick
their lips and salivate: my body a shining slice
of cherry cheesecake, my breasts twin spaniels
off the leash, the bouncy castle of my thighs.

Despite my strength and speed and near
invulnerability to pain, there's nothing new:
the unpaid labour, crazy hours, saving the world
from *boys will be boys*, one sleazebag at a time.

They dress me up as July the fourth: spangled hotpants,
red-heeled boots, my cape a parody of stars n' stripes.
This bustier? Puh-leeze! Eagle wings unfurl feathers
like fingers, grappling each scarlet, silken boob.

Spiderman and Superman get megabucks for half
the degradation I endure. No rule to *smile* for them,
no imperatives for warmth, no spinning themselves
on the tanning bed, kebab meat on a spike.

I was given my script from birth, rehearsed
for the role from *It's a girl!*, trained to preach our
need for female solidarity while whirling my tits
around like mushroom vol-au-vents on a tray.

Fuck that. I want to take up room. I want to spread
my legs on the subway, hurl my voice, to scowl
whenever the hell I please. It comes to this:
I want to meet the eye of any man and feel no fear.

Get me scotch on the rocks, my coffee hot, get me
the biggest slice of key lime god-damn pie you've got.
Go, apprehend your creeps. I want my sweetbreads
skinned and a big white bed that's empty save for me.

starlings

in the beginning is the skydeep
and the skydeep is shapeless and hollow
and blankness dwells there
and the bodyus broods over the belly of the horizon
    clinging to skeletons of trees
                    and we say let there be wavetrail
                    and there is wavetrail
                and we divide the wavetrail from the skydeep
                and the outpour from the inshrink
                        and we call the wavetrail WE ARE
                    and we call the skydeep IT IS
            and we say let there be curlsmoke in the midst of the skyswim
and let it divide the WE ARE from the IT IS
                and we fashion the curlsmoke from the skyswim
                    and it is so
                and we call the curlsmoke ONE
                and the skyswim we call MANY
        and we say let the breakwave be heard among the MANY
                and the pebblerush also
            and we call the breakwave FLESH
                and the pebblerush we call SPIRIT
                    and thus it is
then we say let the SPIRIT be divided into the skybright
    we will call LIGHT and the outsnuff we will call DARKNESS
    and let DARKNESS bring about a great shitting upon the earth
and we say let DARKNESS herald
    the downpull and the stenchsweet,
    the dirtroost and the clutchheart
                and so it goes
            glory be to the skydeep and the bodyus
                the curlsmoke and the skyswim
            glory be to the breakwave and the pebblerush
                the dirtroost and the outsnuff
                for we are the MANY
                we are the ONE

Self-Portrait with Julia Roberts's Hair in 'Pretty Woman'

I dream it's mine, wear it long and loose,
let its curls flicker around my face, its auburn
river course down my back, my shoulders, neck.
This hair gives me sass, allows me to sing to Prince's
Kiss in a bubble bath, to say *Big mistake. Big. Huge.*
to snooty salesgirls. It is Natalie Cole belting out
'Wild Women Do'. It's why I'm poised in this tight
red dress, long white gloves, diamonds at my throat,
posed with opera glasses, crying beautifully on cue
at the climax of the action. Which is to say, this hair
stands right on the balancing beam between sexy

and classy, beachy waves and too-tight perm. In my
dream, hair like this sees me through a trip to the races
and, simultaneously, a sexual assault. It buys me a golden
ticket to a fancy meal with complicated cutlery with which
I will fire a snail across the dining room, say *Slippery
suckers aren't they?* and be thought cute. Ultimately
my hair will make a rich businessman lose his shit/come
to his senses/understand it's *me* who's saving *him*/impel
him to drive in an open-top, white Lincoln limo to claim me
like his raffle prize. It will permit me to say with conviction
I want the fairy tale and get the fairy tale, dammit.

The Life Model's Union Representative Shows her the Ropes

Try to get a kip in, if you can. Nod off to the slap
of clay on board, the soft click of the church hall
clock, the slippered tread of the teacher on his rounds.
Fan heaters will belch their niff of singed-dust
disapproval. Some days, when they're propped too far
away, your nipples stand on end. Others, they're so close
your arse'll scorch. Attempt a quip, *Put the chips on, pal,*
I'll be ready in half an hour. That'll get a grin.

What a crew. Remember, they're not interested in you.
All they want can be taken away to shore up on their walls.
Not sex, exactly. Possession. You can feel it crackling
like cash as you slip off your robe. It's there
in the way they size you up, eyes sliding past your cellulite,
their longing for beauty pert as a paintbrush grasped
in an outstretched fist. Don't fret. After that first,
long-famished look, they'll barely glance your way.

Sometimes, when you come to, a stalactite of drool
will drip from your chin onto the sheet. Other times,
you'll snore. It could be worse. Maeve once woke
to the sound of her own fart ricocheting
round the room. Not much phases her these days.
Mind, you'll need to keep your nerve when schoolkids
caw like crows at the window, when your blimmin' hip
hurts so much you'll bite your lip and count the minutes.

But I'll teach you all the tricks: how to cut your tampon
strings on period days, how to spot the beardy 'nudist'
up for anything but art. Pub work's worse
on half the pay, I always say. Here, you can limp
to the loo on coffee breaks, rub the leg that took
the weight, gather your unseen self to you again. Yeah.
Time moves slow. You'll stir with limbs so numb
it's hardly human. Try to get a kip in, if you can.

Matryoshka

We're all in the family way. Full of ourselves.
In the pudding club, my dear.
On our shelf, we gather dust like snowfall
and listen to the sound of human children
growing. Their girls — once born —
are great squishy, smelly things that pule
and puke and shit the sodding bed.

Not ours. We are a nest with all our pretty
chicks inside. We are the hatchling
and the egg. Each of us is mother
to a daughter who is pregnant
with the next in line. Our bodies rhyme,
like the faces of the moon.

All except our smallest.
We don't talk about it but
let me say it softly:
she was born with no space
inside. That's right.

She's wood all the way
through. It's not that we
judge her, understand, but
we know (as only

mothers can)
she'll never get to split
herself in two,

she'll never have
to bear the others

as we do.

In which I imagine my aborted foetus sings to me

when i was a bird   inside your body's cage of gold
i'd swing   umbilical   bound by a fibre's span
 i ate your bread   drank from your communion
    cup   i was bright new bones and blood

when i worshipped   it was in your chapel   slipping
and soaring   in a pool of stained-glass light
 listen to me   i have known paradise
    have learned by heart   your heartbeat's song

in your garden   it was always summer and i
stitched myself together   under the apple tree
 no fruit forbidden   no act unclean
    for that quickening time   you were entirely mine

i was your well-wound spool   your coil of line
        that binds

Preparing Sunday Lunch with Nan-Nan's Ghost

She's busy doing though she's been dead, what,
twenty years? In her kitchen's fragrant haze
she measures flour and milk by eye, beats
the batter with a fork, flexes her wrist
to pour it in the dimpled tin, hot fat
pooling in its cups. She knows her Yorkshires
will rise like clouds, knows the meat will ascend
from the oven, bronzed as her arms that time
in Vegas when she hit jackpot on the slots.

Grandad's here. He's dead too, bored to death
by dementia, daytime telly, sippy cups.
He snores on the sofa, startles to, scans
Ceefax for the football scores. Mum, Dad —
our Jean, our Alan — are in the front room,
still young, still married, still miserable,
though they'll outlive us all. I'm six, nit-combed
from the night before and bathed in Mr Matey,
sat ringside as Nan-Nan lifts aloft

the joint of glistening beef from the cooker's
eyelash-singeing blast of heat. She anoints
the flesh with oil. The pressure cooker valve
jitters, hisses over the stove's blue flame.
Inside, the cabbage yields. But it's later
I'm waiting for, after the meal, the time
when she and I will stand at the sink
together, washing up: the radio's gabble,
her soft body near and warm as I wobble

on my plastic step. Spoons will glint through
the suds as we baptise a past that hasn't
happened yet: where Nan-Nan doesn't let
recriminations fly, tribal round Mum's
head, where Dad didn't decide to leave, became,
instead, a better man. In the afterlife
where they live now — the one that's shortly
to be mine — all will be transfigured. We'll scrub
those plates like silver dollars, make them shine.

Knitting Nan-Nan

I cast her on with double-pointers, Sheffield Steel.
First, I do her slippers in shabby, worsted wool,

alternate rows of knit and purl. Then up the tan
support stockings that always rib around her ankles.

Her shins are fiddly — their cabled veins require another
(same-gauge) needle, slipping stiches back-and-forth.

I pause for a mug of tea, a Custard Cream, before I tackle
the vast, loose landscapes of her hips, belly, thighs.

My needles click like tiny typewriters and she spools
from them — her Fair Isle of stretchmarks, her bingo wings.

I knit the screeching polyester dress she wore to clean
the step, knit her freckled hands, her wedding band, knit

the tumour nestling in her breast. When I reach the last stitch
of her blue-rinse shampoo and set, she casts herself off.

Now, she lies in my lap as I once did in hers: her neck's
soft crepe, that trace of B&H, the shrill acrylic of her voice.

My Grandparents Pose on the Steps of St Matthew's Church Sheffield, Boxing Day 1942

They live in a box under my bed, hypnotised
in black-and-white. Ken, the butcher's boy with a grin
that won the meat raffle, and Mary in her parachute-silk
dress, conjuring a horseshoe in one hand —

Ta-dah! — like a rabbit from a hat. And though his suit
is far too large across the shoulders, though his neck
is nipped by a too-tight tie, though his teeth buck
at crazy-paving angles, here they are, joined.

Tall in heels, she has slid her hip into the gap
his waist makes — their young marriage slick as the trick
of the lady sawn in half and spun around on stage,
magicked together by a smug, black-cassocked priest.

Petals of confetti fleck her hair and lie at both
their feet. She's Queen of this ring, riding
the gleaming white horse of her wedding day
bareback, her veil gliding out behind

and not my Nan-Nan as I saw her last — snoring
on the ward, bedecked in winceyette, dentures
gurning in a glass by the bed — cast adrift
in a soft and slack-mouthed sleep.

On a Wicksteed Rocking Horse, Grindleford Playground, Sheffield, Summer 1979

That's me: the girl with a pudding-bowl cut,
red-and-white checked polyester dress, three
buttons sewn down my bib, the cabled cardie
Nan-Nan knitted to match. My tummy's full

of contraband KitKat, her part of the deal
as she lights up a Silk Cut — *Don't tell
your Grandad, duck.* Then she's lifting me up,
up above the tarmac's petrol-shimmering heat,

placing me in state at the helm
of a steel stallion. My tiny fists grip
his bridle as Little Ted lolls behind in the first
of four passenger seats. The horse's eyes

widen, nostrils flare. He grits down on the black bit
between his teeth. In the background, some boy charges
towards an invisible ball. Nan-Nan holds the camera,
takes the snap. Freeze frame. In this suspended

quarter-second, my small form is the Atlas
rocket that blasted off from Cape Canaveral
that June. I don't know Thatcher's snatched
victory; the Winter of Discontent remains

a mystery to me as does China's new, one-child
rule. For heaven's sake, I've not even started
school, haven't hovered alone at playtime's edge
nor felt the asphalt's dismal stare. I haven't

learned how to hide behind my hair in class
nor cower in the library at lunch. Here, though,
now, I grin so hard my cheeks are the fat
baked apples we'll eat — *for after us tea* —

and my smile's so wild my eyes are squished
sultanas. I'm the froth on this gallop's
neck, this rolling, roiling flight. Look closely.
Something impossible is happening:

the horse's features fuse with mine, my body
forges to his. I stretch each sinew, roar
— *I'm ready!* — ready for the ride towards
a world I believe has built itself for me.

Flamingo

My love, when I die, I'll turn flamingo:
fall asleep, face tucked in on the pillow
of myself. Even as you cry, I'll be stepping
from the bed, feeling plush, pink tulle tutuing
from my hips. My legs will telescope, grow
thin and rosy. I'll sense my feet web, feel
a new itch to stamp and stir, to suck up
larvae from the bottom of the lagoon.

In this afterworld, some days I'll fix
one foot in mud, find infinite repose:
the poise of a yogi in prayer. Others,
I'll gorge myself, filter feed on brine shrimp
from the salty shadows. The other birds
and I will grunt and growl over the choicest
cuts like church women bickering
over rosettes for jam at a country show.

My love, do you know that the dead all flock
together? We meet at the saline lake, dance
our shuffle-legged shimmy, flick our heads
like tango partners, flag and flap our
scarlet scalloped wings, heads bopping, nodding
to the beat. Do you see? After the illness,
after the grief, the pain — as you will do,
sweetheart — the dead must learn to love again.

Acknowledgements

Thanks to the editors of the following, where some of these poems first appeared: *The Poetry Review, The Times Literature Supplement, Poetry Wales, Magma, Poetry Ireland Review, The London Magazine, Mslexia, Wasafiri, Butcher's Dog, Bad Lilies, Banshee Lit, iamb, The Interpreter's House, Under the Radar, The Friday Poem, The Alchemy Spoon, The Fenland Poetry Journal, Words for the Wild, The Aesthetica Anthology, The Verve Poetry Press Anthology of Poems on Beginnings, The 2021 Hippocrates Prize Anthology, The Broken Sleep Books Ecopoetry Anthology, Christmas Stories: Twelve Poems to Tell and Share* (ed. Di Slaney and Kathy Towers, Candlestick Press: 2022), *21 Poems About Wonky Animals* (Candlestick Press: 2023), and *Weddings: 10 Poems* (ed. Kathryn Bevis, Candlestick Press: 2023). Several of the poems in this collection were published in my pamphlet *Flamingo* (Seren: 2022).

'My body tells me that she's filing for divorce' was shortlisted in the 2023 Forward Prize for Best Single Poem – Written; 'My Cancer as a Ring-Tailed Lemur' was one of the twenty recorded winning poems for The Poetry Archive's Archive Now WordView Collection, 2023; 'Song o' the River Itchen' was highly commended in the 2023 Aesthetica Poetry Prize (a competition that welcomes previously published work); and a portfolio of poems, 'Anniversary', 'Rehab vs. Palliative Chemo: A Service User's Comparative Analysis', and 'Everyone will be there' was highly commended by The Manchester Poetry Prize, 2023. 'Delinquent', 'Teddy', '2020', and 'My Grandparents Pose on the Steps of St Matthew's Church Sheffield, Boxing Day 1942' were published by *Magma* in their Solitude issue as part of their Selected Poet series. 'Translations of Grief' won the Wales Poetry Award, 2022. A portfolio of five poems that appear in this collection (including four previously published poems) was joint winner of the Belfast Book Festival's Mairtín Crawford Award for Poetry, 2022. They were: 'Matryoshka', 'Knitting Nan-Nan', 'The Darkening', 'Delinquent', and 'My body tells me that she's filing for divorce'. 'The title of this poem is "What's the Title of this Poem?"' was one of the winners in The Poetry Society's *Poetry News* Members' Competition, Summer 2022; 'My body tells me that she's filing for divorce' won first prize and 'My Cancer as a Ring-Tailed Lemur' won second prize in the Second Light Competition, 2022 (a competition that welcomes previously published work). 'Egg' won the inaugural Crysse Morrison Prize, Frome Festival, 2023. 'Anagrams of Happiness' won the Poets & Players competition, 2019, under the title 'HAPPINESS' and 'starlings' won the Against the Grain Competition, 2019. 'Song o' the River Itchen' came second in *The London Magazine* Poetry Prize, 2023, 'Wonder

Woman Questions Her Status as a 70s Symbol of Female Empowerment' came second in the Poets & Players Competition, 2022, 'This' came joint second in the Edward Thomas Poetry Competition, 2022, and 'Preparing Sunday Lunch with Nan-Nan's Ghost' won second place in the Poetry, Prattlers and Pandemonialists Competition. 'A Wedding' was highly commended in the Ver Poets Competition, 2020, and an earlier version of 'How Animals Grieve' was highly commended in the Wells Poetry Competition, 2022, 'The Clearing' was commended in the Ver Poets' Prize, 2019, 'In this poem, your routine bloods have come back normal' was commended in the Hippocrates Prize, 2022; 'Matryoshka' was commended in the Hippocrates Prize, 2021; 'Flamingo' was commended in the Second Light Competition, 2022; 'Knitting Nan-Nan' was commended in the Verve Poetry Festival Competition, 2021. 'You will survive' was shortlisted for the Oxford Brookes International Poetry Competition, 2021, 'Knitting Nan-Nan' was longlisted for the National Poetry Competition, 2022; 'Flamingo' was shortlisted for the Bridport Prize in 2022, 'Anniversary' and 'On a Wicksteed Rocking Horse, Grindleford Playground, Sheffield, 1979' were shortlisted for the Bridport Prize 2023.

I am grateful thanks to the Hosking Houses Trust for their award of a residential to complete this body of work in the early weeks of 2024.

Sincere thanks to all my teachers, mentors, and poet friends who've work-shopped and edited these poems with me or have inspired me deeply in other ways. They include: Jo Bell, Robyn Bolam, Carole Bromley, Dillon Jaxx, Vanessa Lampert, Kim Moore, Ewan Monaghan, Isabel Rogers, Clare Shaw, and Robert Walton. Heartfelt thanks to all the members of The Circle and The Wonky Animals' Collective.

Profound thanks to my editors at Seren, Zoë Brigley and Rhian Edwards, for their unwavering belief in my work and for their skill and patience. Thanks to the whole team at Seren, from production to design and market-ing and for producing this collection within limited time.

Warm thanks to Vicky Morris for her shrewd and skilful line edits to so many of these poems. Affectionate thanks to my mentor, colleague and friend, Jonathan Edwards, for helping me conceive, shape, order and edit so many of the poems in this collection. Without him, this collection wouldn't exist.

Loving thanks to Ollie for being exactly who you are, for being everything to me.

Note

All the poems in this collection are in conversation with other poets and poems, seven of them particularly so. Special thanks to: Andrew Waterhouse, whose 'Climbing my Grandfather' inspired 'Knitting Nan-Nan'; Greta Stoddart, whose 'You Drew Breath' helped me to frame 'You will survive'; Nick Laird, whose 'The Given' inspired 'The Smuggler'; Richard Evans, whose 'Murmuration' I responded to in 'starlings'; Fiona Benson, whose 'Dear Comrade of the Boarding House' helped me to frame 'In this poem, your routine bloods have come back normal'; and Dorianne Laux whose 'Heart' inspired 'Love'. Sincere thanks to Caroline Bird, who set a version of the first line of 'Teddy' as a prompt in one of her workshops. The refrain in 'This' is a quotation from Johann Wolfgang von Goethe.